A PLACE OF MY OWN

Johan, Hana, Ratheena and Sami have found some magical wellington boots. When they put them on, they are transported to wonderful and comforting places, and even through time. Where will they take you?

With growing concerns around mental health, and in the wake of a period of uncertainty and change, it is more important than ever to pay attention to how young children express their emotions and to teach them to articulate their thoughts in a healthy way. This beautifully illustrated picture book has been created to inspire conversations about safe spaces, helping practitioners assess a child's mental health competency and helping the child visualise a place to which they can escape when they feel anxious and upset.

When it comes to child and adolescent mental health issues, prevention and early intervention are key. The 'serve and return' format of this book provides a virtual space where children can explore thoughts and feelings and teaches them a coping mechanism that can be used in the future to escape negative thoughts.

Louise Jackson is a teacher, trainer and author who draws on her direct experience of working with children in schools to develop educational materials that are designed to promote participation, relationships and conversation. She has worked on 'closing the gap' projects with national charities, local authorities, schools, children's centres and training organisations to address educational disadvantage, finding new ways to build capacity and resilience across early childhood services and local communities.

Privileged to have worked alongside many inspirational teachers, practitioners and volunteers in educational settings where vulnerable children are thriving, Louise seeks to capture in her research and writing what it is that makes the difference for young children. Working in collaboration with illustrator Katie Waller, she has created a series of books and practical tools which will help local communities, parents, practitioners and teachers understand the valuable role they can all play in cultivating resilience in early childhood.

A practical guide for early years practitioners
and four children's picture books to
use with 4–6-year-olds.

A PLACE OF MY OWN

A Thought Bubbles Picture Book About Safe Spaces

Louise Jackson
Illustrated by Katie Waller

Routledge
Taylor & Francis Group

LONDON AND NEW YORK

Cover image credit: Katie Waller

First published 2022
by Routledge
2 Park Square, Milton Park, Abingdon, Oxon OX14 4RN

and by Routledge
605 Third Avenue, New York, NY 10158

Routledge is an imprint of the Taylor & Francis Group, an informa business

British Library Cataloguing-in-Publication Data
A catalogue record for this book is available from the British Library

Library of Congress Cataloging-in-Publication Data
Names: Jackson, Louise, 1964- author. | Waller, Katie, illustrator.
Title: A place of my own : a Thought Bubbles picture book about safe spaces
/ Louise Jackson ; illustrated by Katie Waller.
Description: New York : Routledge, 2022. | Summary: A magical pair of boots
transports Johan, Hana, Ratheena, and Sami to wonderful, comfortable places.
Identifiers: LCCN 2021028280 (print) | LCCN 2021028281 (ebook) | ISBN
9781032135816 (pbk) | ISBN 9781003229964 (ebk)
Subjects: CYAC: Space and time--Fiction. | Imagination--Fiction. | Security
(Psychology)--Fiction. | LCGFT: Picture books.
Classification: LCC PZ7.1.J328 Pl 2022 (print) | LCC PZ7.1.J328 (ebook) |
DDC [E]--dc23
LC record available at https://lccn.loc.gov/2021028280
LC ebook record available at https://lccn.loc.gov/2021028281

ISBN: 978-1-032-13581-6 (pbk)
ISBN: 978-1-003-22996-4 (ebk)

DOI: 10.4324/9781003229964

Typeset in Madeleina Sans
by Deanta Global Publishing Services, Chennai, India

It's cold and dull
and there's nothing to do.

STOP!

Look here.

What's this? What can you see?

A pair of boots in
a golden light!

Who do they belong to?
Not you? Not me!

What
should we do?

Put them on ...
Oh but I'm not sure?

Do you think that
we can?
We should?
Or we might ...?

Johan was first to step out with courage.

He wriggled his toes and took a deep breath ...

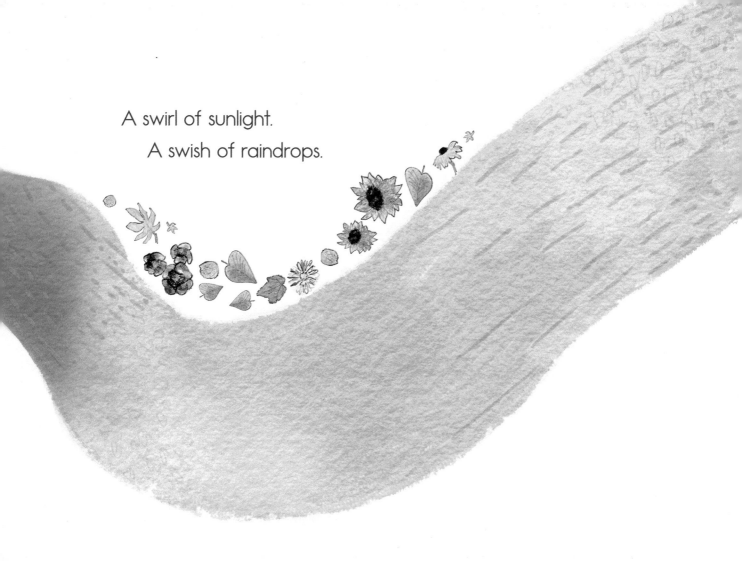

A swirl of sunlight.

A swish of raindrops.

Johan turned
around and around
and was whisked
far, far away ...

Johan stepped out into a dense, dark forest.

Tall trees,
squawking birds,
creepy crawlies
and a carpet of
flowers.

Along came Hana, to have a go.

A swirl of sunlight.

A swish of raindrops.

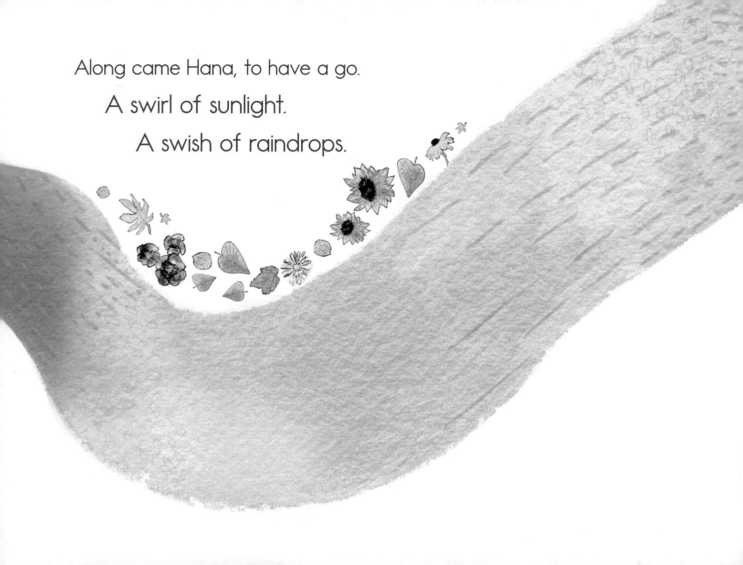

Hana turned
around and around and
was whisked far,
far away ...

Hana stepped out,
with snow underfoot.

A wooden hut with a welcoming light, mountains and fir trees, a snowy sight.

Along came Ratheena, to take her turn.

A swirl of sunlight.

A swish of raindrops.

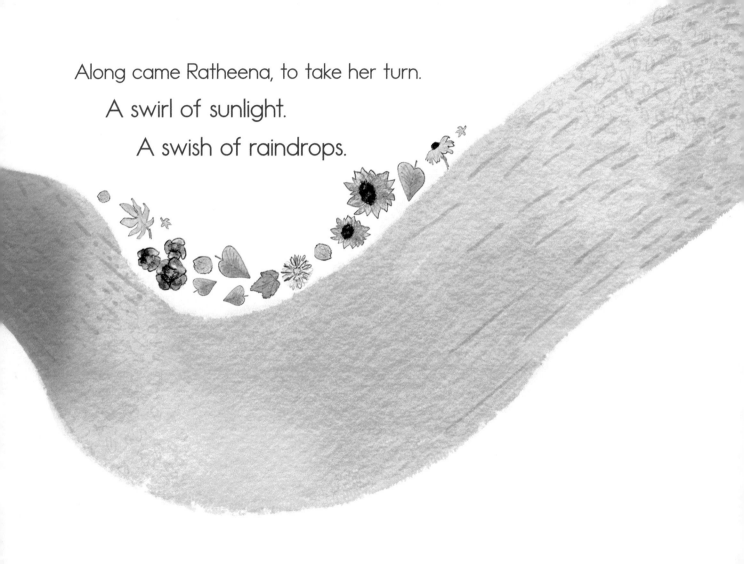

Ratheena turned
around and around
and was whisked
far, far away ...

Ratheena found
that she had stepped back in time.

The sounds, smells and people she knew oh so well.
A place she remembered, her friends were there as well.

Sami wasn't sure if she wanted a go, but before she could say no ...

A swirl of sunlight.

A swish of raindrops.

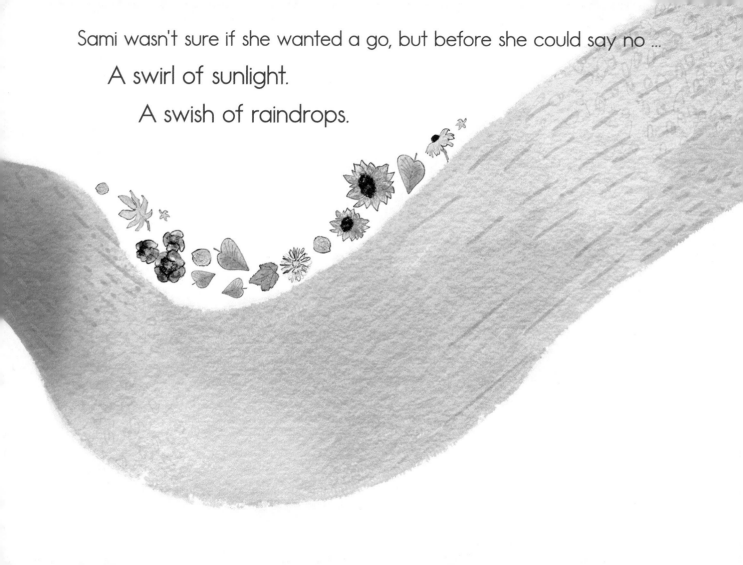

Sami turned
around and around
and was whisked
far, far away ...

She found herself in
the garden at home.

All together again,
Mum, Dad, her dog and
the baby there too.

She smiled at the memory, it was time for their tea!

So now it's your turn, step into the boots and shut your eyes tight ...

A swirl of sunlight.

A swish of raindrops.

Turn around
and around.
You'll be whisked
far, far away!

I wonder
what you'll find?